CAPTAIN
Sir Tom Moore

ONE HUNDRED REASONS TO HOPE

Illustrated by
Adam Larkum

CURATED BY
Danielle Brown

INTRODUCTION BY
Hannah
Ingram-Moore

PUFFIN

D1320132

Contents

Dear reader,

My father loved nothing better than hearing people's stories and marvelling at unexpected courage. When we were growing up, my father would say, 'Don't just talk about the weather. Ask people an unknown fact about themselves. Then you'll find out who people really are and their lives will probably surprise you.' These stories of unexpected courage, of everyday people, have done just that. Always wanting to inspire hope in others, my father would have pored over this beautiful book for hours, breathed in every word and smiled at every illustration.

Reading about these extraordinary, everyday heroes is a reminder of how incredible the human spirit is. Of how, during the pandemic, so many people did their best to be brave, show empathy, be thoughtful and support each other. Emotions would soar and deflate in a matter of moments, and small gestures carried enormous weight and could change the lives of people we barely knew. We saw parents digging deep to teach subjects they hardly remembered from school, while simultaneously trying to cling on to their incomes. We saw doctors and nurses putting patients above their own personal lives. We saw frontline workers keeping the country going, day in, day out. All generations, from old to young, demonstrated how resilient, innovative and creative we all are. It is hard to believe all that has taken place in one year.

When my father set out to walk one hundred lengths of our garden, none of us could have predicted what happened next. Those simple steps turned into something quite extraordinary and during his walk, my father received so many letters and emails from people going the extra mile and helping others. He spoke to some of them on Zoom calls; he even met a few in the brief lockdown easing of summer 2020. Some of these people are in this book, and Danielle and Adam have brought these incredible stories to life in these pages. When we spoke together about the idea of this book, my father was delighted that these incredible people would get the recognition they deserved. We are proud to celebrate them with his blessing, and many other everyday heroes, in this book of hope for the future.

The support my father, and my family, received during his last year was extraordinary; after he raised money for the NHS COVID-19 appeal, we would be stopped in the street by strangers, asking us what we would be doing next. My father said he would like to continue to help raise funds, to support those who have little and who need help. My father's life had been difficult at times and he understood how small gestures helped, so together we set up The Captain Tom Foundation to raise funds to support all that he believed in, such as equality and supporting mental health.

With a twinkle in his eye and a huge smile on his face, he would be delighted that this book shines a spotlight on people who have done extraordinary things during the pandemic, and thrilled that it supports The Captain Tom Foundation. While the pandemic has shown us how tenacious we can be, I know that there has been much loss and pain during this time. But we will get through difficult times by believing, as my father did, that by taking one small step at a time, tomorrow really will be a good day.

Hannah Ingram-Moore

Throughout the course of human history, we have faced many different viruses and infectious diseases, which can be tricky to control and can cause disruption on an extraordinary scale.

A new virus, which caused an infectious disease called Covid-19, spread around the world in 2020. It became a pandemic: an outbreak of a disease which quickly infects many people, and spreads over a wide area. There are still lots of unknowns, and scientists are trying to learn more about the virus. It was first noticed when people became ill with flu-like symptoms, and before long the same virus was found across the world. We think that the first cases of Covid-19 reached the UK at the end of January 2020. All viruses mutate and different variants of Covid-19 now exist.

The world needed to work quickly to try and contain the virus, and different countries tried different approaches. In the UK, we were told to wash our hands, stay inside and socially distance ourselves. For some time we lived with changing restrictions, such as lockdowns and not being able to go to school. Throughout the lockdowns, key workers put themselves at risk to keep the country running, and scientists raced against time to find out more about the virus so we could better protect ourselves.

But it wasn't just the virus that travelled around the globe. Hope did, too. We saw acts of kindness as strangers supported one another, people raised essential funds for charities, and communities worked together. It wasn't always easy to stay hopeful, but hope was found in the most unexpected places. We saw that no person is too young – or too old – to make a difference. We don't know what the future holds, but there are reasons to be hopeful. So here are one hundred reasons to hope: true stories of everyday courage, kindness and perseverance. Stories of inspiration, of working together, and of hope – to remind us that storms will always pass.

is always the hardest,
that first step you'll never finish.'

– Captain Sir Tom Moore

When Covid-19 spread across the UK, many NHS staff – including doctors, nurses, cleaners, care workers, paramedics and pharmacists – worked round the clock. They put themselves at risk from the virus to help their patients.

HASSAN AKKAD A CLEANER IN THE NHS

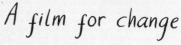

A film for change

Hassan Akkad is a filmmaker, author and activist. In 2015 he fled from the war in Syria and came to the UK as a refugee, winning a BAFTA award for the film he made about his treacherous journey. When the pandemic began, Hassan wanted to help his community, so he started working as a hospital cleaner. Dressed from head to foot in PPE, he scrubbed and disinfected the ward to keep the virus at bay.

This was a dangerous job, but NHS cleaners and porters born outside the UK got no support for their families if they died from the virus. So Hassan recorded a heartfelt video asking the government to change this law, and thousands of people got behind Hassan's message. Within hours of the film being shared online, the government agreed to support all NHS workers, no matter what job they did, or where they came from.

No job is too small to make a difference

As the UK stood on the brink of the pandemic, the NHS looked to medical students to join the ranks of staff preparing to fight the virus. Chanelle Smith was one of 2,213 students who volunteered to help. While still at university in her fifth year, she helped junior doctors with essential tasks, from taking blood to filling out paperwork.

NHS HERO

Evening News

OUR HEROES
NHS

From the other side
of the world

One doctor travelled 10,000 miles to do her bit for the NHS. Layla Guscoth is not your average doctor. She's an international netball player, too, and she was playing in Australia when the pandemic struck. She managed to travel back to the UK, swapped her sports kit for scrubs, and threw herself into thirteen-hour shifts.

THANKS
NHS

Doctors on call

Alexander Finlayson is a GP and also an entrepreneur. When patients needed to stay at home, he wanted to find a way to continue their treatment. So his company created the Nye Phone, a video platform that lets doctors speak to their patients remotely, keeping everyone connected and safe. Named after Aneurin 'Nye' Bevan, the founder of the NHS, Alexander let doctors and nurses use the app for free.

2020 NEWS

The nurses of Ward 25 at the Queen Elizabeth Hospital, Gateshead, cared for people with Covid-19. To help their patients dream of beating the virus, they decorated a board with a gigantic rainbow. Every patient who was well enough to go home added their name in a bright yellow star. It was a reminder that even in a crisis, there is hope.

> A little bit of kindness is the key to getting through this.

A nurse for life

After forty-two years working as a nurse, Catherine Fitzsimmons retired from the NHS. Just a year later, she was back in her uniform working on the Covid-19 frontline. The NHS urgently needed more doctors and nurses, and Catherine was one of the first to step forward. She helped her patients keep in touch with their families when they had to stay apart.

Your NHS needs you

More than 15,000 former doctors and nurses agreed to start working for the NHS again.

The birthday must go on

Balloons and bunting decorated the staffroom, but they weren't for the doctors or nurses. Dr Rory Nolan's daughter, Francesca, was celebrating her first birthday. Rory was a trainee GP and had decided it was too dangerous to live with his family in case he brought Covid-19 home. His colleagues knew how much he missed his family and today was a special birthday. So when Rory arrived at work, they surprised him with cake, sandwiches, cards and presents. They celebrated Francesca's birthday despite being far apart, and hoped for their future reunion.

When the people of the UK were told to stay at home, it was hard to know how to help. Annemarie Plas had an idea: Clap for Our Carers, a small act of appreciation for those battling the pandemic. She invited the entire nation to clap, cheer and make some noise from their doorsteps.

LOCAL

Daily Gazette

Communities who clap together

For the first ten weeks of lockdown at 8 p.m. on a Thursday, you could hear applause across the country. From small streets to major cities, we banged pots, rang bells, cheered and clapped as a small mark of our appreciation.

School's out

As the last bell rang on Friday 20 March 2020, millions of children across the UK walked out of the school gates and didn't come back until the start of June. Schools shut again from January to March 2021. Both times, Covid-19 was spreading fast and schools closed to everyone except the children of key workers as part of the national lockdowns to reduce infections.

Learning at home was very different, and many students felt lonely away from their friends and teachers. Pupils had to learn in different ways, and some even uncovered new skills, such as seven-year-old Amelie Thurman. She learned how to DJ and, after putting on a virtual gig for family and friends, was invited to DJ on BBC Radio 6 Music. Eleven-year-old Lydia Johnson missed her theatre group, so she performed songs from the musical *Oliver!* in an online concert for charity.

A team of teachers

Gerry Robinson works as a headteacher in one of the most deprived areas in London, and the pandemic hit her school hard. She opened a food bank at the school, spending hundreds of pounds of her own money to make sure her students and their families had enough to eat. Other teachers joined in, helping to pack and deliver food parcels. Gerry also loaned school laptops to students who didn't have a computer at home, and posted out homework so that nobody fell behind.

One small classroom, one large class

Primary school teacher Ashley Bates was worried that children would miss out on their education when schools closed. He wasn't sure how he could help, but when he was clearing out his garden shed he had an idea – this would make the perfect classroom! Mr Bates opened The Shed School, and from Monday to Friday you could find him live-streaming free lessons from his shed with help from his mischievous sidekick, Mr Monkey. From his tiny classroom, Mr Bates helped more than 4,000 students practise their English and maths together.

From hospitals to schools, supermarkets to transport, postal deliveries to bin collection, and many more essential services, there are more than 7.1 million key workers in the UK.

A milkman on a mission

'In all my years as a milkman, I have never let anyone down - and I don't intend to now,' said Tony Fowler, who went far beyond delivering milk. Many of his customers were over the age of seventy and didn't feel safe going to the shops, so Tony picked up food, toilet rolls and prescriptions for them and delivered them to their doors.

An unexpected delivery

The streets were quiet during the lockdown of spring 2020, so postman Jon Matson thought he'd deliver a smile on his postal round. Every day he donned a different fancy dress outfit. One day he was an ancient Greek soldier, another day a chimney sweep, and he was even a postbox. His community looked forward to spotting him, especially five-year-old Macey, who started dressing up too. On the last day of lockdown, Macey dressed as a postal worker, just like Jon.

A new recipe for success

Dawn Butler is an award-winning baker. She's made cakes for royalty and celebrities, but when the pandemic began she took on a new challenge. She decided to squeeze in a second job, so each morning Dawn got out of bed at 3 a.m. and headed to a supermarket warehouse. Here she packed online orders, getting them ready to be delivered. Once her shift was over, she went home to run her baking business, and gave free cake-decorating lessons in lockdown.

More than 136,000 extra staff were taken on by supermarkets at the beginning of the pandemic to keep shelves stacked, stores clean and help with the big increase in home-delivery orders.

Blue-light emergency teams

Firefighters across the UK teamed up with the NHS to drive ambulances. This helped paramedics to treat more patients and put more ambulances on the roads, caring for those who needed it the most.

Free rides

Many taxi drivers, including Robert Malcolm from Glasgow, gave free rides to NHS staff, taking them to and from their hospital shifts.

The boogieing binmen

Waste collectors Jack Johnson, Henry Wright and Adrian Breakwell wanted to spread a bit of joy in their neighbourhood during lockdown. Using wheelie bins as props, they performed in the street. One dance routine became two, which became three . . . videos of the Dancing Binmen throwing their best moves went viral. The three friends also released a Christmas song, 'Boogie 'Round The Bins At Christmas Time', raising money for local charities.

Five postboxes outside hospitals were painted blue to thank NHS workers for their efforts. A postbox near Captain Tom's home was also painted blue for his one-hundredth birthday.

A message to deliver

Eight-year-old Tallulah Mclellan waited on her doorstep for delivery driver Tim Joseph. He regularly dropped off parcels at her house and when Tallulah realized he was deaf, she wanted to learn sign language. One day she surprised him. 'Have a good day,' she signed when he reached the garden gate. Tim was delighted. He taught her how to sign 'Good morning', and the pair have been friends ever since.

The next stop is . . .

One of the passengers on Alex 'Alec' Bailey's bus burst into tears. For the first time in months, Jacqueline Mason was going to visit her mum in her care home, but she'd got on the wrong bus by mistake. Alec told the other passengers that he was going to take a small detour, and changed his bus route. Thanks to Alec's kindness, Jacqueline arrived on time and was reunited with her mum.

'You can do and be

anything you want.'

The world's biggest PE class

During the first week of lockdown, Joe Wicks bounced on to our screens, ready to lead us through a fitness workout.

Joe wanted to help children stay active when schools closed, and lying in bed that night, the idea came to him: PE with Joe. The next day, he invited families all over the country to join him at 9 a.m. on Monday 23 March 2020 for a virtual PE lesson. He wasn't sure how many people would turn up. He certainly wasn't expecting more than 800,000! People tuned in from all over the globe, and on the Tuesday he broke the world record for the biggest live-streamed YouTube workout.

'I'm going to be the world's PE teacher for as long as you need me,' Joe said, and every morning from Monday to Friday he Spider-Man-lunged, kangaroo-hopped and duck-walked across his living room. His energy was infectious and whole families joined the feel-good sessions. In total, Joe ran more than seventy sessions, which were viewed more than 80 million times. Together his PE classes also raised over half a million pounds for the NHS.

Time to draw together

You don't get an art lesson from a real-life illustrator every day, but these weren't ordinary times. During lockdown, illustrator Rob Biddulph invited families to draw with him. Step by step, he taught us how to draw our favourite characters from his books. These sessions were so popular that Rob smashed the world record for the largest online art class, while raising money for the NHS.

Music in the streets

Professional cellist Romain Malan was used to performing in grand concert halls. But when his audiences could no longer go to events, Romain brought his music to them, swapping the stage for the streets. He organized more than one hundred small street concerts across the UK, matching local musicians to people who were self-isolating to lift the spirits of those indoors.

Quiz the nation

Every Thursday night, Jay Flynn and his friends took on their local pub quiz. When the pubs closed, Jay had an idea: why not host a virtual quiz of his own? It was only supposed to be a small gathering . . . but over half a million people said they wanted to come! Each week, Jay became the nation's quizmaster, breaking the world record for the largest online quiz and raising over £1 million for charity.

Follow the rainbow

Fed up of hearing bad news, Crystal Stanley wanted to bring a bit of brightness to her community. In Italy, pictures of rainbows were appearing in windows, and Crystal thought she would try this in Ipswich to cheer people up on their daily walks. Her daughter, Ariana, helped her paint a big, beautiful rainbow and they displayed it in their window. Crystal asked other people to help make a Rainbow Trail.

The colourful signs of hope caught the Queen's attention too.

'The moments when the United Kingdom has come together to applaud its care and essential workers will be remembered as an expression of our national spirit, and its symbol will be the rainbows drawn by children.'

In April 2020 the Queen made a rare TV appearance, sharing a message of hope and comfort.

Soon rainbows were spotted all over the town and, as word got out, people across the whole world joined in. The idea spread positivity as rainbows of all sizes popped up everywhere. Some people created paper-chain rainbows, mosaics, street paintings and some families even coloured in the bricks of their houses!

A new story for a long lockdown

J.K. Rowling's unpublished story, *The Ickabog*, had been sitting in her attic
for ten years, but now she was ready to share the fairy tale with the world,
one chapter at a time. She asked children to illustrate the story,
and soon drawings came flooding in. Thirty-four winners
had their illustrations published and J.K. Rowling
donated her royalties to charities supporting
people affected by Covid-19.

Time to listen

At the beginning of lockdown, children's
author David Walliams entertained readers with his wickedly
wonderful stories. Each morning for thirty days he released a
free audio story, encouraging families to listen together.

A day at the museum

Sacha Coward and Dan Vo work to make
museums exciting, so when they closed their doors,
they decided to take the public on virtual tours
instead. Visitors could peek behind the scenes and
see how museums were looking after their
collections, and together the duo inspired people to
talk about their favourite museum artefacts.

Painting portraits

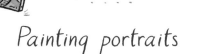

Tom Croft wanted to capture the spirit of the NHS staff, and
came up with Portraits for NHS Heroes. He offered to paint a
free portrait of an NHS worker and asked other artists to join
him. Requests flooded in, and Tom matched more than 500
painters with doctors, nurses and paramedics. Worldwide,
thousands of paintings have now been produced.

hine on you again and the clouds will go away.
tomorrow will be a good day.'

One hundred steps

Ninety-nine-year-old Captain Tom Moore set himself a challenge. He wanted to raise £1,000 by walking one hundred lengths of his garden before his one-hundredth birthday. It was an ambitious target, but Tom was determined to give it his best shot.

Eighteen months earlier, he had fallen and broken his hip. In hospital, he received the very best care and Tom never forgot the kindness of the NHS staff who nursed him back to health. Now Tom wanted to show his own support for the doctors and nurses who were risking their lives to save others.

As the sun shone down, Tom walked back and forth in his garden with his trusty walking frame. It took four days to reach his £1,000 target and people began to take notice. Tom's story was shared around the world and messages of support – as well as donations – came flooding in. It didn't take long before thousands of pounds became millions, and Tom kept walking.

On his one-hundredth lap, Tom was saluted by a guard of honour from the 1st Battalion of the Yorkshire Regiment. This was Tom's regiment when he served as an army captain in the Second World War.

When he found out he had raised more than £12 million, Tom was delighted. 'It's completely out of this world,' he said, and he vowed to keep walking for as long as the donations kept coming.

The final total came to a whopping £38.9 million, which broke the world record for the most amount of money raised for a charity walk.

On Tom's one-hundredth birthday, he received more than 200,000 birthday cards. Later, he was even awarded a knighthood from the Queen! Tom appreciated the kindness and generosity that people showed him on his big day.

Tom *didn't set out thinking he'd make such an enormous impact, but he discovered that*

one step has the power to inspire one hundred more . . .

Captain Tom captured the nation's imagination and inspired others to raise funds for charities . . .

Another step

With the help of some scaffolding poles, Mike Biggar lifted himself from his wheelchair and took a small step forward. He was determined to walk one hundred steps in thirty days. Mike was captain of the Scotland rugby team in his youth, but finds walking very difficult after a serious car crash. Before starting the challenge Mike could manage four steps at a time, but it wasn't long before he could do more and he smashed his target in just seven days – and set himself a new challenge of 500 steps! He completed this, and reached almost 2000 steps.

A ginormous challenge

A marathon is 26.2 miles long. The furthest Tobias Weller could walk was fifty metres, but he was determined. Tobias has autism and cerebral palsy, and as he walked up and down his street with his orange walking frame, he became a familiar sight. Soon Tobias worked up to 750 metres a day, walking until he'd walked a marathon. Not content with one marathon, Tobias set his sights on a second . . . fifty-two miles and 110 days later, Tobias crossed the finish line again. He was joined by Olympic gold medallist Dame Jessica Ennis-Hill who he had challenged to a race.

Step by step

The Evelina London Children's Hospital saved Tony Hudgell's life when he was a baby, after he suffered serious injuries that meant both his legs were later amputated. Seeing Captain Tom on TV inspired five-year-old Tony to set his own challenge and, after getting new prosthetic legs, he decided to walk ten kilometres. One step, then another, and another. With the love and support of his adoptive family, Tony completed his epic walk throughout June 2020 and raised more than £1.3 million for the Evelina Hospital so they can look after other children.

Keep on, keepy-uppy

Ten-year-old Imogen Papworth-Heidel decided to do one keepy-uppy for every key worker in the UK. She started with 200 a day, but with 7.1 million key workers, Imogen realized it would take 97 years to finish. This would make her even older than Captain Tom! She asked others to donate keepy-uppies and more than 2,000 people joined in, including Marcus Rashford, Lucy Bronze and other England players. Carefully counting every keepy-uppy, Imogen's challenge was completed in seven months. Imogen managed a whopping 1,123,586 keepy-uppies herself, sometimes knocking out 7,000 in a single day.

Taking on mountains

During the Second World War, Margaret Payne climbed Suilven, a mountain in the Scottish Highlands. At ninety, she took on the peak once again – this time from her own home, climbing the 731 metres by walking up her stairs 282 times.

A walking wonder

Covid-19 restrictions meant that 104-year-old Ruth Saunders couldn't hold her annual coffee morning to raise money for charity. That didn't stop her . . . she walked a marathon instead. When Ruth completed her challenge, she had a message for Captain Tom: 'Tom, I've done it!'

Running together

During the first lockdown, Olivia Strong noticed more people out running, and she had an idea – why not start a charity challenge? Her idea was Run for Heroes: run five kilometres, donate £5 to the NHS and nominate five friends to do the same. Soon it went viral, and people from all over the world ran seven million kilometres and raised £7 million, together.

A marathon mindset

Each year, the streets of London are taken over by thousands of determined runners. But in 2020 only elite athletes were allowed to run the official London Marathon course – everybody else had twenty-four hours to run a marathon in their local area. And so, on Sunday 4 October, more than 43,000 people across the country took part in the first virtual London Marathon. Running together but apart, they raised over £16.1 million for charities.

The highs and the lows

Sometimes people can feel happy, and at other times they might feel low, depending on their mental health. Sally Orange wanted to emphasize these highs and lows by running in the highest and lowest locations. So Sally ran her virtual London marathon on a treadmill in a London Eye pod, 135 metres above ground. Six days later she ran another marathon, but this time it was 1,000 metres underground, in a mine in North Yorkshire.

An adventure for a friend

Before Rick Abbott passed away from cancer, he gave his ten-year-old neighbour Max Woosey his tent and made him promise to have an adventure in it. Max wanted to raise money for North Devon Hospice, who had cared for Rick, so he decided to find adventure in his own garden – and camp through the first lockdown. But that wasn't the end of his adventure . . . 365 days later, Max was still camping, sticking it out through hot summer days and icy wind, rain and snow. When he'd been camping for one year, he invited children to join Max's Big Camp Out, camping in their own gardens or living rooms. Max raised more than half a million pounds in honour of Rick – and he still shares his friend's love of adventure.

The 2.6 fundraiser

Fundraising events had to be cancelled during the pandemic, and charities lost a lot of vital donations. So on Sunday 26 April 2020, volunteers across the country took part in the 2.6 Challenge and raised over £11.2 million for charities. Any activity could be sponsored as long as it was based around the numbers two and six: read twenty-six books, walk 2.6 kilometres, bake twenty-six cakes, or lead an online workout with twenty-six friends.

A teammate's challenge

Seven is an important number for Kevin Sinfield. It was the number of his former teammate, Rob Burrow, when they played rugby league for Leeds Rhinos together. After Rob was diagnosed with motor neurone disease (MND), Kevin challenged himself to run seven marathons in seven days to raise £77,777 for Rob and other families with MND. He smashed his fundraising target on the first day and by running, and running, and running . . . he raised more than £2.7 million.

When work becomes home

In March 2020, on the second day of the first lockdown, a team of nine carers packed their bags, said goodbye to their families and moved into the care home they worked at.

Together they worked long shifts every day of the week to look after the twenty-three residents at Bridgedale House. The team slept in spare rooms or on blow-up air mattresses in the communal training room.

The team chose to do this because they didn't want to risk bringing Covid-19 into the care home, or taking it back to their own homes. There were no Covid-19 cases at Bridgedale House, partly due to the actions of the team.

Laughter in lockdown

Older adults were most at risk from Covid-19 so, during the peak of the pandemic, care homes were closed to visitors to help keep residents safe. Quarantining like this could be lonely, but the staff at Bryn Celyn Care Home in Wales found a creative way to keep everybody entertained. They played a real-life game of Hungry Hippos with four residents in wheelchairs. The care home filled with laughter as they tried to collect as many coloured balls as they could in baskets on long sticks.

Going above and beyond

In Keighley, the same town where Captain Tom grew up, Samantha Faulkner cares for people with learning disabilities. One of the residents she looks after, Rhiannon Norris, became unwell and needed to go to hospital. Samantha stayed with Rhiannon and slept on the floor next to her hospital bed, making sure Rhiannon got the care she needed. When Rhiannon was well enough to go home, they self-isolated together as a precaution to make sure they didn't pass the virus on to anybody else.

A distanced disco

After eight weeks of lockdown, the residents of Burgh House Care Home in Norfolk were missing their families. The staff had an idea: a drive-through disco! Music blasted through the speakers as residents lined up outside the care home, waving Union Jack flags and dancing. Families and friends slowly drove through the car park, giving them a chance to see their loved ones from a safe distance.

'Because one step has the power

to inspire one hundred more!'

Healthcare workers wear personal protective equipment (PPE), special clothing that stops germs from spreading. PPE is one of the best defences against Covid-19, but hospitals didn't have enough to go around. Across the nation, volunteers rallied together to help solve the PPE shortage.

Scrubbing up together

The hospital where Ashleigh Linsdell worked as a nurse didn't have enough scrubs – the uniform that medical staff wear. Ashleigh turned to social media, asking for help finding fabric. Hundreds of people wrote back! Ashleigh set up a Facebook group called For the Love of Scrubs and organized her volunteers. From the Shetland Islands to the southernmost tip of Cornwall, people stitched for the NHS – together, more than 70,000 volunteers made over one million sets of scrubs!

Secondary schools across the UK donated safety goggles and rubber gloves from their science labs to help with the PPE shortage.

Pocket money for PPE

In the Easter holidays, Nahla-Rose Bartlett-Vanderpuye borrowed her grandma's 3D printer. She had a plan: to make visors for NHS staff. Nahla-Rose used her pocket money to buy materials and set up a mini factory on her dining table. She practised and practised until she could print a visor in just over an hour. She donated over 1,000 visors to local hospitals!

Make your own

Wearing a face mask is important, but ten-year-old Millie Millburn didn't want a boring mask. She wanted her mask to show her love for gaming, art and heavy metal, so she chose material decorated with skulls and blue roses. Her mum taught her how to create a mask, and it looked so good that people wanted their own – which was the beginning of Millie's Masks. In a few weeks, orders were coming in by the thousands, and Millie and her mum had to bring in extra staff!

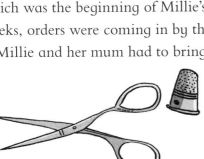

Caring for the community

Toilet roll, hand sanitizer and soap got snapped up at the beginning of the pandemic. When Asiyah Javed found an elderly woman crying outside the supermarket because all the hand soap was gone, Asiyah knew she had to do something. She runs a corner shop with her husband, Jawad, and together they ordered hand wash, masks and disinfectant wipes, and made hundreds of free care packages for vulnerable people in their community.

Add some colour

Six-year-old Patrick Dixon has a condition called cystic fibrosis, and long before Covid-19 he wore a mask to protect himself from germs. Patrick realized that PPE might seem scary for children who aren't used to it. Armed with his mum's sewing machine, he joined a volunteer group, stitching colourful masks for NHS staff and care homes.

Stop the spread

Ninety-two-year-old Connie Diggle spent her evenings on the faithful sewing machine that she got in 1947, making scrub bags. These helped healthcare workers take their dirty uniforms home and put them straight in the wash without spreading the virus.

An abundance of volunteers

During the first few months of the pandemic, some of the most vulnerable people had to shield, which meant they couldn't leave their homes. The NHS needed 250,000 volunteers to provide a lifeline by picking up prescriptions and food, safely driving people to doctor's appointments, and making phone calls to help with the loneliness. In only four days over 750,000 people signed up, ready to help.

Time to volunteer

Nine-hundred hours – or thirty-seven and a half days – is the amount of time that Simon Bucknell clocked up as an NHS volunteer. He squeezed this in around working fifty hours every week as a cycling delivery driver. But he didn't stop there – Simon set up a fundraising campaign to buy sandwiches for NHS staff at his local hospital.

A helping hand

Arif Voraji runs a charity, Help the Homeless, that feeds, clothes and finds housing for homeless people in Leicester. During the pandemic, homeless people were given emergency accommodation in hotels and houses. Arif worked hard to make sure that they had toiletries, bedding and other essential items. He also realized many other people needed help, and delivered food parcels to anybody in the community who needed one.

A helpful harvest

In 2017, Oliver Bailey's son, Henry, was born with spina bifida. A team of surgeons at King's College Hospital London performed a seven-hour operation that enabled Henry to walk. Oliver was grateful for the NHS's help when his family needed it and he wanted to do something for medical staff in their time of need.

At the beginning of the pandemic, supermarket shelves emptied quickly. NHS workers, who often finished work at times when supplies had already run out, found it tricky to buy groceries. Oliver came up with the idea of Harvest for Heroes, bringing boxes of fresh fruit and vegetables to local hospitals so staff had food to take home. He teamed up with his friends and local food suppliers, and within two weeks they had raised more than £25,000 and delivered healthy food boxes to fifteen hospitals across London and the south-east.

Calling at the hospital

Jolene Miller switched from working as a paramedic to a train driver two years before Covid-19 spread across the world. But when the UK was preparing to go into the first lockdown, she knew her medical skills would be needed again. So she drove trains one week and volunteered at her local hospital the next week. Jolene found out what care patients would need as soon as they arrived at hospital, waiting with them until a room became free.

Dig for dinner

In 2020, Farmer David Walston had an idea to help with any food supply problems: if farmers worked with local communities, they could grow fresh, healthy food for everybody. He turned some of his fields into giant vegetable patches, inviting neighbouring villagers to grow food together. They had a bountiful harvest and donated spare fresh produce to charities and the NHS. David himself delivered a big box of vegetables to the paramedic who saved his life in 2019 when his heart stopped beating after a cardiac arrest.

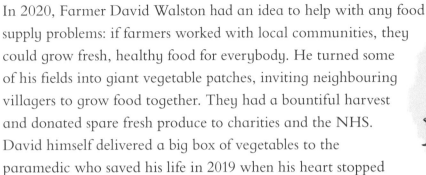

Growing with the garden

In the middle of bustling Bristol, an old wasteland has blossomed into a thriving garden. Tara Miran's community garden was a place for people to relax – and it became especially important in the pandemic. This green, rambling place gave hope to its community, who could escape here to grow fruit and vegetables, exercise and enjoy the peace.

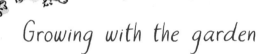

Air to breathe

During the spring 2020 lockdown, there were fewer cars on the roads and planes in the sky. In some UK cities, air pollution dropped by up to 60%, making the air we breathe cleaner and healthier.

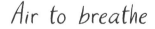

Singing in the silence

Cities, towns and villages fell quiet through the
lockdowns, yet the birds seemed to sing louder . . .
or did they? Scientists discovered that birds were
actually singing more quietly, but with fewer cars
on the roads we could hear their songs more
clearly – songs that had been there all along!

Sharing our cities

As cities became quieter, it became easier to spot some
wilder city residents. Endangered leatherback sea turtles
were counted in greater numbers on empty beaches in
Phang Nga, Thailand, laying their eggs without being
disturbed by large crowds. And in San Francisco, USA,
sparrows in the city started to sing different tunes because
they didn't have to shout over the traffic to be heard.

Looking up in lockdown

With more people staying at home, there were fewer man-made lights to wash out the sparkling
night sky. Stargazers reported clearer skies above us, counting more stars in the quiet of lockdown.

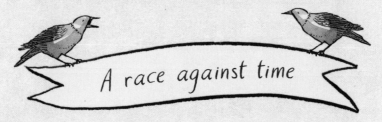

A race against time

During the first peak of the pandemic in spring 2020, there was a risk that hospitals could run out of beds and ventilators. Temporary hospitals were swiftly constructed and named Nightingales, after the nineteenth-century nurse, Florence Nightingale.

It took only nine days to transform ExCeL London from an exhibition centre into a hospital for 500 patients. This took a humongous effort: each day, up to 200 soldiers worked side by side with NHS staff, electricians, plumbers, carpenters and engineers to build the world's biggest pop-up hospital. The soldiers worked fifteen-hour shifts and together the team laid floors, constructed cubicles and set up medical equipment so the hospital would be ready, with room to add a further 3,500 beds if they were needed.

Nine other Nightingale hospitals were built around the UK in a race against the rising number of Covid-19 cases. Building the NHS Nightingale hospitals in a handful of weeks was an incredible feat, and was only possible because different experts worked together to make it happen.

Leading the team

Colonel Ashleigh Boreham only had a few weeks left in the army before he retired when he got a call asking him to oversee the construction of the Nightingale hospital in London. He had led medical units in the military so he knew how to organize building temporary hospitals, but this was a project on a much, much larger scale. Ashleigh worked closely with the NHS and they mobilized the teams to get it done.

Help for home haircuts!

As the weeks of the spring 2020 lockdown turned into months, the nation's hair became more and more shaggy. Some people resorted to giving their own hair a trim, including Dan Silvertown. It did not go well. This gave Dan and Jeroen Sibia, his business partner, an idea to save the nation from DIY haircut disasters. They created Lockdown Haircut, the UK's first virtual barber, where professional barbers talked people through a home haircut via a video platform. This helped barbers to work remotely, and the profits went to NHS charities.

Choose your own handwashing song

Do you remember when we were told to sing 'Happy Birthday' twice when we washed our hands? Seventeen-year-old William Gibson felt sad singing a celebration song over and over again, and wondered if there was another way. He built a website, Wash Your Lyrics, so people could choose a song they liked to sing while washing their hands for the recommended amount of time. It combined the lyrics in a poster with step-by-step handwashing instructions. Over four million posters were downloaded from William's site, making handwashing a little bit more entertaining.

Connecting a digital world

Covid-19 changed the way we connect with the world almost overnight. Peter Paduh knew the impact technology can have: when he came to the UK as a refugee in the 1990s, he was given a second-hand computer while he lived in foster care. He never forgot this kindness, which helped him to start a career in IT, and since then he has supported others who couldn't afford a computer. In 2020, he asked businesses to donate any spare laptops and tablets to the elderly, homeless and vulnerable, keeping hundreds of people connected to the world around them.

A drone delivery

The Isle of Mull takes almost an hour to reach by boat from mainland Scotland. In May 2020, the island got the chance to test out a brand-new delivery system: drones dropped off Covid-19 tests and PPE four times a day. This trial could help remote communities access medical supplies more quickly in the future.

Keeping in touch

While we're far apart, we can still stay close: the number of people in the UK making video calls every week doubled during the spring 2020 lockdown, from 35% to more than 70% in April 2020.

47

STORIES OF KINDNESS

'Above all, be kind.'

Working for results

When Erin Bleakley went to collect her grades on results day, she got a nasty surprise: they were much lower than her teachers had predicted. She had worked so hard and was worried that this would ruin her chances of becoming a vet. As exams had been cancelled, the system that decided grades affected those who lived in deprived areas much worse than those from more affluent areas. Erin organized a student rally and carried a banner with the words 'JUDGE MY WORK, NOT MY POSTCODE'. Together the students helped change the system so grades were decided by teachers who knew what students could achieve in an exam, rather than where they lived.

The community cuppa

Many people felt lonely during the pandemic, and when one lady mentioned she was finding it hard, her whole street in Hebden Bridge, Yorkshire, worked together. Neighbours sat in deckchairs outside their houses so they could all have a socially distanced cup of tea and chat, letting her know that she was not alone.

Letters for lockdown

During lockdowns, having very little contact with the outside world could be lonely, so sixteen-year-old Nina Andersen started Community Senior Letters. She matched care homes with primary schools, whose students wrote letters and drew pictures to lift the spirits of care-home residents.

'A small act of kindness, such as sending a letter, can make the world a better place.'

Write it on a postcard

Becky Wass had a simple idea to allow communities to help each other: she made postcards, asking whether her neighbours needed any help if they were self-isolating, from a friendly phone call to fetching shopping. She shared the postcard template on social media so others could post them to their own neighbours, spreading a little bit of kindness.

Neighbourhood superheroes

Even Spider-Man had to get his daily exercise to stay fit and strong during the national lockdowns – and children in Stockport spotted the superhero running past their windows while they stayed at home. Friends Jason Baird and Andrew Baldock took it in turns to dress up as Spider-Man on their daily jog, raising spirits in their town as they backflipped outside houses and waved to those inside. 'Spidey Stop Here' posters appeared all over town as children requested a visit to their street, and the superheroes raised over £50,000 for the NHS.

Giving back

'Can we not all agree that no child should be going to bed hungry?' wrote Marcus Rashford in a letter to Parliament. The words came straight from the heart, and from memories of a time when he relied on free school meals and food banks. His mum, Melanie, worked hard to provide food for her family, but sometimes there hadn't been enough to go around.

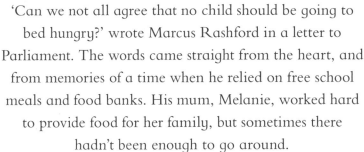

Marcus, now a spectacular striker for England and Manchester United, had not forgotten the generosity of the people in his community who helped his family. Many children were going hungry during the Covid-19 crisis, with over 200,000 children missing meals when schools closed. Marcus used his voice on behalf of all the children who received free school meals, asking the government to continue the scheme during the summer holidays. And it worked: vouchers for meals were given to these pupils.

Marcus raised more than £20 million for charity to feed schoolchildren during the lockdowns, and brought supermarket chains and charities together to push the government for a long-lasting solution. Alongside his football training, Marcus continues to campaign against food poverty in the UK.

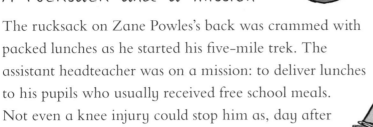

A rucksack and a mission

The rucksack on Zane Powles's back was crammed with packed lunches as he started his five-mile trek. The assistant headteacher was on a mission: to deliver lunches to his pupils who usually received free school meals. Not even a knee injury could stop him as, day after day, he powered through the glorious sunshine of the first school closures and the dreary winds and rain of the second. Zane's daily trips meant he could check his students were safe, and he delivered more than 15,000 meals.

Chefs for change

At the beginning of the pandemic, one in six children in England relied on free school meals. Nicole Pisani is a chef and when the first national lockdown began, she wanted to help children who were going hungry. She quickly raised funds to make food hampers for families who needed them. From school kitchens to restaurants, her team of volunteers cooked and delivered over 80,000 meals.

Sharing the celebration

120 guests were invited to celebrate Fiona and Adam Gordon's wedding, which they'd spent more than a year planning. But due to Covid-19 restrictions, the party couldn't go ahead. They got married anyway, but didn't want all the party food to go to waste . . . So the newly married couple donated it to their local hospitals in Hull, providing 400 warm meals to NHS workers.

Goody bags for carers

Wearing layers of PPE and washing their hands again and again during long shifts left hospital workers with broken and chapped skin. Lauren Ezekiel, a former beauty editor at a magazine, had a plan. She knew people who could donate skincare products to the NHS – and the response was overwhelming. So many items were donated that she had to hire space in a warehouse to store them all! More than 20,000 goody bags were given to hospitals.

Knitting for the NHS

As the army built the Nightingale hospitals, Margaret Seaman was working hard on the NHS Knittingale. She wanted to find a way to do her bit for the NHS, but at the age of ninety-one, she couldn't go out to volunteer so she stayed inside and knitted . . . and knitted, and knitted, stopping only to eat her meals. Thirty-four balls of wool and three months later, she had crafted an entire hospital from wool to raise money for her three local hospitals in Norfolk. The NHS Knittingale had an A&E department, three wards, a helipad, fifty-eight knitted figures, and it all sat beneath an enormous rainbow.

2020 HAPPY NEWS

Happy news from around the world

It was easy to focus on bad news when the pandemic disrupted our lives. Friends Manon McAllister and Eva Spickernell decided to create their own newspaper, *Happy News*, which only featured positive stories. The eleven-year-olds had weekly video calls to discuss the content and researched each topic thoroughly, writing hopeful reports every week, from a double rainbow in Scotland to two boys finding gold in their garden in France. *Happy News* was available for free through their village's shop and helped their community remember positive stories, however small or large.

Pedal power

Pedalling through the streets of east London, Emdad Rahman was on a mission to bring happiness to his communities and share his love for reading. Supplied with donated books, he cycled far and wide, sometimes as far as thirty kilometres a day. Named Bookbike London, Emdad delivered to care homes, homeless shelters and families, supplying them with books and a cheery smile.

Bags of love

When the tooth fairy left five-year-old Amaya Thompson some money, she knew exactly how she wanted to spend it: making 'bags of love' for homeless people. She filled twenty bags with food, toiletries and a thoughtful letter, hoping her gift bags would bring a smile. Amaya didn't stop there – she set up a fundraising campaign so she could make more bags of love for the homeless, hospital workers and teachers at her school.

STORIES OF HOPE

'The trick is to

walk on with hope in your heart.'

We will beat this together

Tuesday 8 December 2020 was a very special day. At 6.31 a.m., before the sun had risen over Coventry, nurse May Parsons administered the vaccine to Margaret Keenan. A quick jab and it was over. Wearing a cheerful blue T-shirt and a gigantic smile under her mask, Margaret was one week away from her ninety-first birthday. She'd just become the first person in the world to receive a vaccine made by pharmaceutical company Pfizer, and she described this as the best early birthday present she could wish for. After spending most of 2020 on her own, she could now look forward to being reunited with her family in the new year.

It was cause for cheer. This was the moment that the UK started to roll out its Covid-19 vaccination programme across the country. After months and months of research, a vaccine could protect us from the virus that had caused so much disruption and sadness. NHS staff lined the hospital corridor, clapping loudly as Margaret was taken out of the ward.

'If I can do it, well, so can you,' Margaret told the nation. She hoped other people would see her and be inspired to get the vaccine . . . and they were! By the time she went back for her second dose, more than 800,000 people in the UK had followed her lead.

This jump-started the biggest vaccination programme the UK has ever seen, and gave us hope that brighter times were on the horizon.

NHS

VACCINATION CENTRE

The speedy roll-out of the vaccine started straight away. Moments later, eighty-one-year-old William Shakespeare rolled up his sleeve and became the second person to get the vaccine. (Just like the famous playwright, this William Shakespeare also came from Warwickshire.)

Record time

It usually takes between ten and fifteen years to make a vaccine, but scientists across the world worked around the clock to bring out the Covid-19 vaccine, from idea to injection, in just nine months.

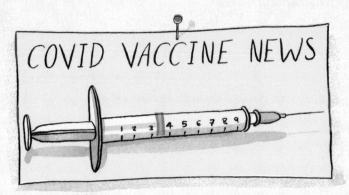

A worldwide effect

The world was counting on the scientific community to find a way to beat Covid-19, so teams of scientists shared ideas across the globe in a way we had never seen before.

Leading the team

Professor Sarah Gilbert led the team of researchers working on the Oxford-AstraZeneca vaccine. She has spent the last twenty years making vaccines for infectious diseases, and she was hopeful that her team could create one for Covid-19. Getting to the lab at the crack of dawn and not leaving until late at night, Sarah and her team were ready to test the Oxford vaccine in fewer than 100 days.

How it works

Covid-19 vaccines work differently but they all do the same thing: they stop us from getting sick by teaching our immune system to detect and fight coronavirus. The three main vaccines first given in the UK were from Oxford-AstraZeneca, Pfizer and Moderna, and all were a huge leap forward in vaccine technology. They cleverly trick our body into thinking we have coronavirus in our system – when we haven't – so it can build a strong defence against the virus.

Volunteers for trials

Scientists needed volunteers to help them test the vaccines. These people were closely monitored by the research team and they kept daily diaries to record how they felt. Over 100,000 people volunteered to take part in the Oxford-AstraZeneca vaccine trial!

The first dose

On Thursday 23 April 2020, Dr Elisa Granato became the first person to receive the trial dose of the Oxford-AstraZeneca vaccine. She was excited to do so because she hoped that this would take us one step closer to getting a working vaccine, which could save millions of lives.

Ready to go

After seven months of trials, the Pfizer vaccine looked promising. It seemed to be doing its job to protect against Covid-19, and the UK became the first country in the world to approve its use on 2nd December 2020. The UK ordered 40 million doses to give to healthcare workers and those over the age of eighty. Shortly after on 30th December, the Oxford-AstraZeneca vaccine was also approved for use.

Rolling out the vaccine

From hospitals to village halls, vaccination sites popped up across the UK to roll out the vaccine at a rapid rate. In just four months, more than thirty million citizens had been given their first dose. That's 179 people vaccinated every minute!

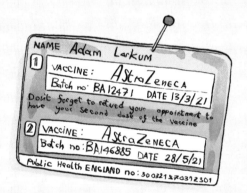

Volunteer vaccinations

In the race to vaccinate as many people as possible, thousands of volunteers were brought in to help the NHS. Mausum Rathod normally worked in TV, but she volunteered straight away with St John Ambulance, and was trained to give the vaccine. She wanted to be part of helping the UK find a way out of the pandemic.

Looking ahead

The Covid-19 vaccine is an incredible breakthrough in medical science. Experts are already looking at how the technology can be used to fight other diseases, sending ripples of hope that future life-saving vaccines aren't too far away.

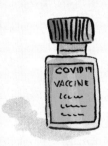

REASONS TO HOPE

In the darkest of times we can still find reasons to hope. Covid-19 cast a long shadow over the world and yet, despite the chaos, confusion and sadness, we found a way forward together.

Across the UK, from the coast to cities and the countryside, we did our bit to protect each other as we hoped for a brighter future. Hope was painted in rainbows and echoed loudly from our doorsteps when we clapped together. We found new heroes in scientists who delivered groundbreaking results in a seemingly impossible timescale. And hope was symbolized by one man, who, on a sunny April morning in 2020, decided to walk one hundred lengths of his garden.

The actions of one person can inspire many, many more. Hope may start as a tiny spark, but when we come together, it grows stronger and blooms into an incredibly powerful force. Throughout the national lockdowns we saw this happening over, and over again. Apart – but not alone – people found inventive ways, both small and large, to spread a smile, lift spirits and support one another. We found moments of joy in everyday things, and we refused to let distance separate us.

Covid-19 has changed our world and there have been difficult days. While we do not know what is ahead, we can choose to remember that we will take these next steps together.

Hope starts with one small step.

And one step has the power to inspire one hundred more . . .

With thanks to the late Captain Sir Tom Moore for his inspiration,
and to Hannah Ingram-Moore, Colin Ingram-Moore,
Benjie Ingram-Moore, Georgia Ingram-Moore,
Adam Larkum, Danielle Brown, Bev James, Megan Carver,
Emily Lunn and Laura Hall

The Captain Tom Foundation was created in response to the most amazing love and support
given to Captain Sir Tom and his family, not only from the Great British public
but around the world, in response to Tom's Walk 100 for the NHS.
The family wanted to create a lasting legacy – the mission:
To Inspire Hope where it is Needed Most
We are supporting causes closest to
the late Captain Sir Tom's heart,
for more information please visit:
https://captaintom.org

PUFFIN BOOKS

UK | USA | Canada | Ireland | Australia | India | New Zealand | South Africa

Puffin Books is part of the Penguin Random House group of companies
whose addresses can be found at global.penguinrandomhouse.com.

www.penguin.co.uk   www.puffin.co.uk   www.ladybird.co.uk

Penguin
Random House
UK

First published 2021
This paperback edition published 2022
001

Printed in China

A CIP catalogue record for this book is available from the British Library

ISBN: 978-0-241-54216-3

Imported into the EEA by Penguin Random House Ireland, Morrison Chambers, 32 Nassau Street, Dublin D02 YH68

All correspondence to: Puffin Books, Penguin Random House Children's
One Embassy Gardens, 8 Viaduct Gardens, London SW11 7BW

MIX
Paper from
responsible sources
FSC
www.fsc.org
FSC® C018179